Dedication

To the enlisted men of the 71st Division Artillery whose loyalty and hard work have brought us to our present readiness for overseas duty, this annual is dedicated.

FRANK A. HENNING
Brigadier General, USA

BRIGADIER GENERAL
FRANK A. HENNING
COMMANDING

COLONEL
GEORGE R. SCITHERS
EXECUTIVE

Hqs. Division Artillery

LT. COL. DONALD H. HENDERSON
S-3

MAJOR D. L. SMITH
S-2

OUR COMMANDERS

LT. ALTON C. EXSTROM
ASST. S-3

CAPT. STOPP   SGT. RYLANCE   LT. ROMAN
S-1   SGT. MAJ.   ASST. S 1

HQS. DIVISION ARTILLERY

"PASS IN REVIEW"

"TALKING IT OVER"

HQS. BATTERY
DIVISION
ARTILLERY

HEADQUARTERS BATTERY

"THIS IS IT"

"GUESS WHO"

BUSINESS AS USUAL

THE GANG

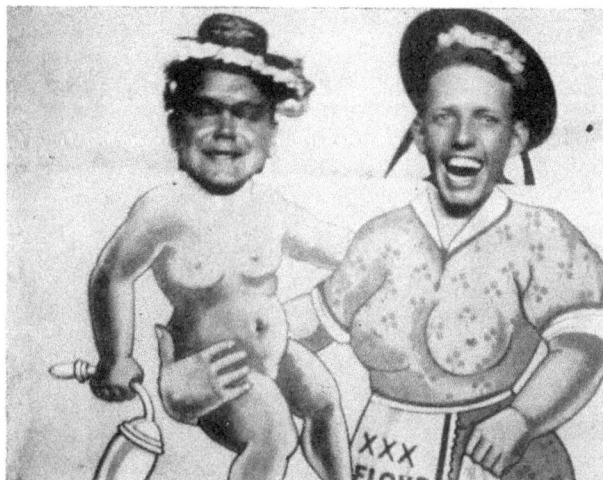

"Chow . . . .

. . . AND AFTER"

CHAPEL

564th
FIELD ARTILLERY BATTALION

LT. COL. CHARLES L. WILLIAMS
COMMANDING

564th

READY

RAM!!

564th

THE SITUATION

RUMMAGE

564 th

"ONE HERE,
ONE THERE"

"ON THE WAY"

"AFTERMATH"

564th

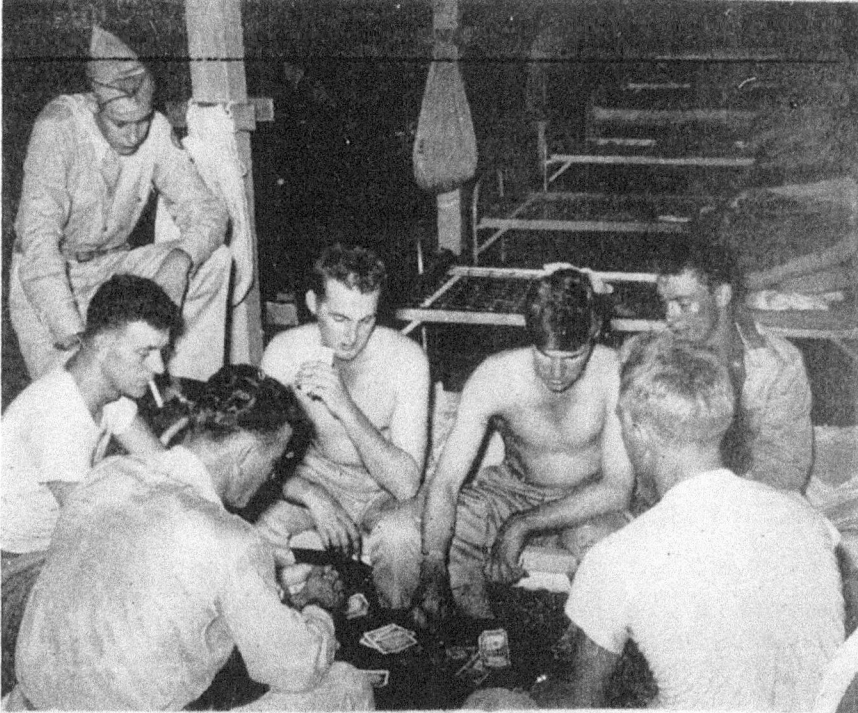

TSK! TSK!

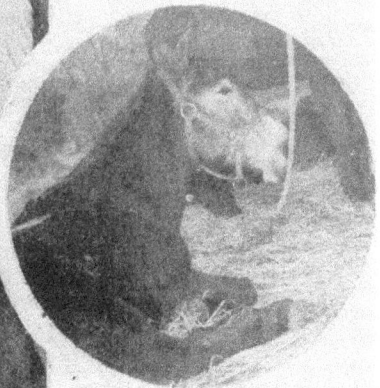

LABOR UNION

OUR HISTORY

On the 14th of May, 1943, the 602nd Field Artillery Battalion completed a march from Camp Hale, Colorado, through the mountains to Camp Carson, Colorado. That evening, the 602nd was divided into two parts. One part remained as the 602nd while the other became the 609th Field Artillery Battalion. Four days previously at Camp Carson the 605th and 604th Field Artillery Battalions were similarly divided and formed the 607th and 608th respectively.

Two months later on the 15th of July, 1943, the 71st Light Division was activated at Camp Carson, Colorado. The 607th, 608th, and 609th Field Artillery Battalions became the artillery of this new division while the headquarters detachment was formed from the Mountain Training Center. During the following summer and fall our battalions trained with the standard light division artillery weapon, the 75mm pack howitzer and its prime mover the army mule. From the 6th of November until the 22nd of January, 1944, the 71st Division went through a combined training period.

On February 6th, the division moved to the Hunter Liggett Military Reservation near Camp Roberts, California. On the 22nd of February, our maneuvers against the 89th Light Division began which were continued until the 29th of April.

After the maneuvers, the 71st Light Division learned that it was to become the 71st Infantry Division and the corresponding necessary changes were started. With mixed feelings, the artillerymen lost their mules and 75mm pack howitzers. The trip to Fort Benning was completed by the 23rd of May, 1944. Soon after our arrival, the light battalions received their trucks and 105mm

OUR HISTORY

howitzers. Each of the thre existing battalions then prepared one battery to go to the firing batteries of a new medium battalion. Additional men were sent from each of the battalions to make up the headquarters and service batteries.

On the 26th of May, 1944, we became the 71st Infantry Division and the 564th Field Artillery Battalion was activated. Battery C of the 608th became Battery A of the 564th. Battery C of the 607th became Battery B of the 564th. Battery C of the 609th became Battery C of the 564th. Men from the 607th, 608th, and 609th Field Artillery Battalions along with the 731st Anti-Aircraft Battalion formed headquarters and service batteries of the 564th. Division artillery headquarters detachment became Division Artillery Headquarters battery.

The primary mission of the Division Artillery, starting the 26th of June, was to execute Field Artillery demonstrations for The Infantry School and the IRTC at three nearby camps. The firing batteries of the 609th left soon after—Battery A to Camp Croft, South Carolina; Battery B to Fort McClellan, Alabama, and Battery C to Camp Wheeler, Georgia. These batteries remained at these posts for two months. All batteries were back with the 71st by September 7th. The Infantry School demonstrations were concluded by our artillery on the 23rd of September. Since that time, the four battalions have trained for and taken battery and battalion tests.

This brings the history of the 564th, 607th, 608th, and 609th Field Artillery Battalions and Division Artillery Headquarters Battery up to November 10, 1944.

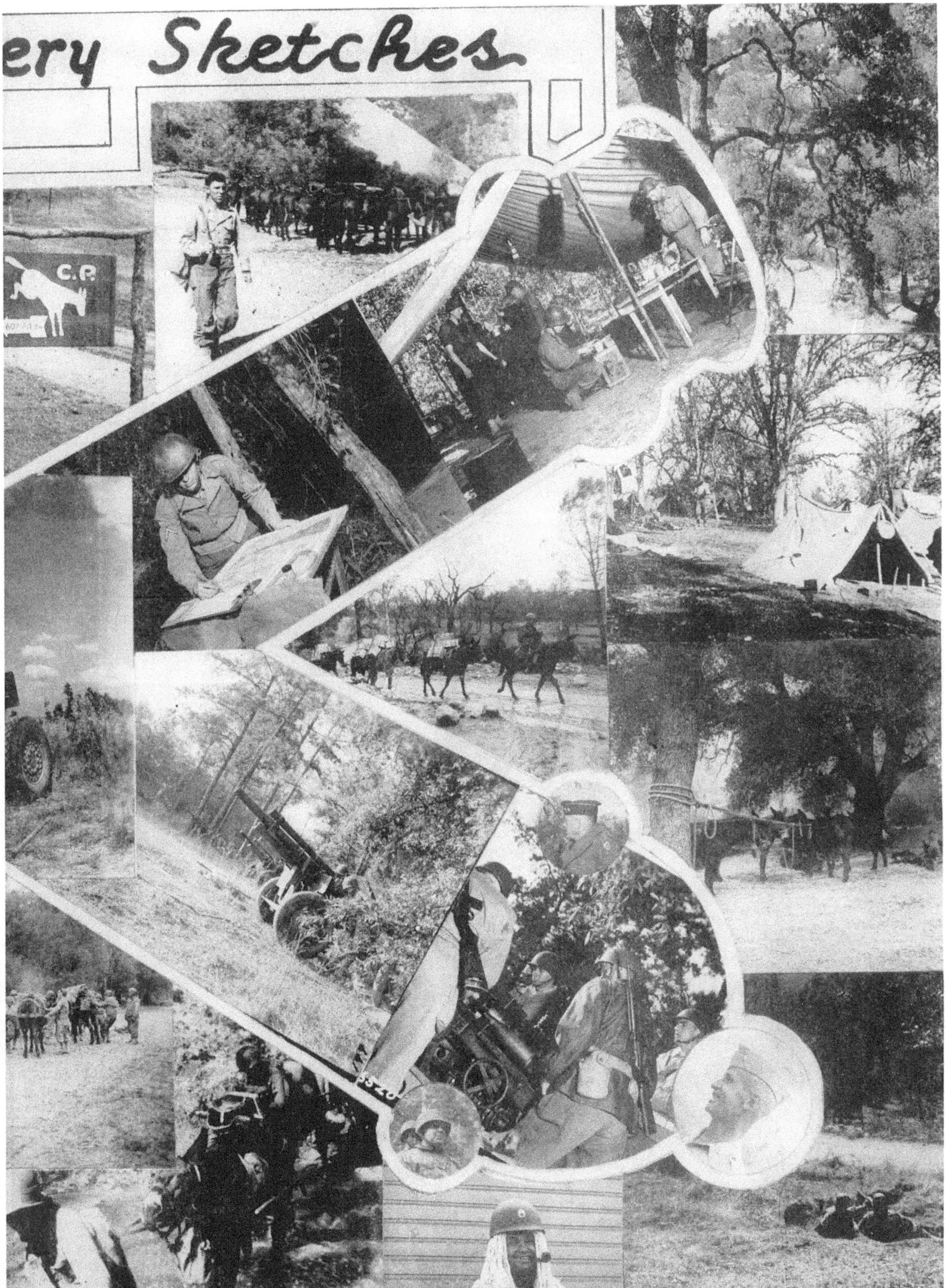
ery Sketches
C.P.

607th
FIELD ARTILLERY BATTALION

LT. COL. GEORGE E. DOOLEY
COMMANDING

607th

UNDERCOVER MEN

CONCENTRATION 19

607 th

"ZERO MILS"

"EAST SIDE, WEST SIDE"

"THE BATHTUB"

607th

"CANNONEERS POST"

"HEADQUARTERS"

"THE CONGREGATION"

607th

"DISH WASHER WANTED"

"FIELD SHAVE"

"BASE CAMP"

GRASSHOPPERS

S. Valdez

608th
FIELD ARTILLERY BATTALION

MAJOR C. W. CLAPSADDLE
COMMANDING

608th

SPIT-N POLISH

DISMOUNT

"TROUBLE?"

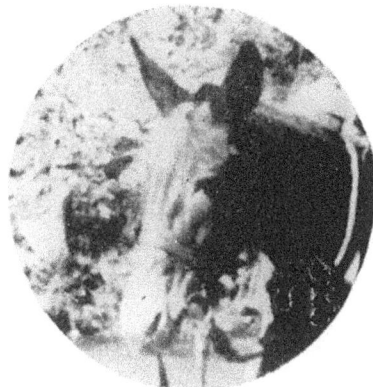

608th

"SEND YOUR MESSAGE"
OVER"

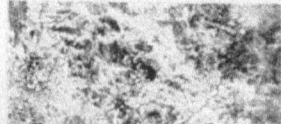

"CHARLIE
OPERATOR"

609th
FIELD ARTILLERY BATTALION

MAJOR ROBERT H. DEASON
COMMANDING

609th

TOP: ANOTHER REPORT!
BOTTOM: WHAT DID YOU DO?

TOP: "ON THE TRAIL"
BOTTOM: OUCH!!

609th

TOP: "PREPARE FOR INSPECTION"
BOTTOM: "SUGAR REPORTS"

TOP: FORWARD HO!
BOTTOM: "SOLID HEAT"

609th

"NAME, RANK, SERIAL NO."

"INSPECTION"

609th

"MY DAY"

"CLEANUP"

REMEMBER...

OUR SINCERE APPRECIATION . . .

to the 168th Signal Photo Company and the U. S. Army Signal Photo Company for their willing and cheerful contributions to the success of this annual.

STAFF

LT. PAUL B. AKIN
LT. JACK R. ROMAN
TEC. 5 S. P. VALDEZ

AUTOGRAPHS

www.ingramcontent.com/pod-product-compliance
Lightning Source LLC
Chambersburg PA
CBHW081159090426

42736CB00017B/3389